Global Criminal Accountability's Grand Pursuit

Charting the course of universal jurisdiction's evolution, highlighting its scope, limitations and contemporary challenges

Lysandra Montgomery

Table of Contents

1 **Introduction: Universal Jurisdiction's Genesis** . . **5**
1.1 Historical Context . . . 7
1.2 Early Applications . . . 9

2 **Defining Universal Jurisdiction** . . . **13**
2.1 Legal Foundations . . . 15
2.2 Jurisdictional Principles . . . 18
2.3 Crimes Covered . . . 20

3 **Scope and Limitations** . . . **23**
3.1 State Sovereignty . . . 25
3.2 Practical Challenges . . . 27

4 **Challenges to Implementation** . . . **31**
4.1 Political Obstacles . . . 33
4.2 Enforcement Difficulties . . . 34
4.3 Resource Constraints . . . 37
4.4 Lack of Cooperation . . . 39
4.5 Judicial Capacity . . . 41

5 **Contemporary Cases & Impacts** . . . **45**
5.1 Notable Prosecutions . . . 48
5.2 Impact on International Law . . . 50

6 **Future Directions** . . . **53**
6.1 Strengthening Mechanisms . . . 55

6.2 Expanding Cooperation 57
6.3 Addressing Impunity 59

7 Conclusion: The Path Forward 63
7.1 Assessing Progress 65
7.2 Looking Ahead 67
7.3 Remaining Questions 70

1 Introduction: Universal Jurisdiction's Genesis

The concept of universal jurisdiction, allowing states to prosecute individuals for serious international crimes regardless of where the crime occurred or the nationality of the perpetrator or victim, didn't emerge fully formed. Its roots lie in the historical struggle against piracy and slavery, offenses universally condemned as violations of fundamental human rights and international order. Early instances, often rooted in customary international law rather than codified treaties, saw states asserting jurisdiction over individuals accused of heinous acts committed far beyond their borders, relying on the inherent authority to punish egregious violations of universal norms. These early applications, while sporadic and inconsistent, laid the groundwork for the more structured approach to universal jurisdiction we see today. The inherent tension between state sovereignty and the imperative to hold perpetrators accountable for the most serious crimes against humanity began to manifest even in these initial instances.

The gradual evolution of international law, spurred by the horrors of World War II and the subsequent Nuremberg and Tokyo trials, dramatically shifted the landscape. The concept of crimes against humanity, previously lacking a clear legal definition, gained sharper focus. These trials, while not explicitly based on the doctrine of universal jurisdiction as we know it today, nevertheless demonstrated the international community's willingness to prosecute individuals for atrocities committed on a massive scale, regardless of national borders or the perpetrator's affiliation. This marked a pivotal moment, signifying a growing consensus that certain acts were so egregious they transcend national boundaries and demanded accountability on a global scale. The groundwork for a more formalized and universally recognized concept of universal jurisdiction was undeniably laid.

However, the path was not without considerable obstacles. The principle of state sovereignty, a cornerstone of the international system, often clashed with the burgeoning idea of universal jurisdiction. States were understandably hesitant to concede jurisdiction over matters traditionally considered the exclusive domain of national courts. The potential for political abuse, the difficulties in gathering evidence across borders, and the considerable resource requirements for prosecuting complex international crimes all contributed to this hesitancy. Despite the early precedent and the undeniable moral imperative, the path forward for universal jurisdiction remained fraught with practical and political challenges. Balancing the pursuit of justice with the principle of state sovereignty was, and remains, a delicate act of international diplomacy and legal interpretation.

The challenge of effective enforcement further complicated the situation. Even when a state asserts jurisdiction, securing the arrest and extradition of a suspect from another nation frequently proved to be exceptionally difficult. Lack of cooperation between states, the reluctance to extradite individuals to countries perceived as politically biased or having questionable judicial systems, and varying legal interpretations across different jurisdictions, all presented significant roadblocks. Many states, for example, argued that universal jurisdiction should only be exercised as a last resort, after domestic courts failed to act or were unwilling to. The inconsistent application of the principle across national jurisdictions reflects this ongoing tension and highlights the need for improved international mechanisms for cooperation.

Furthermore, resource constraints often limit a state's ability to effectively investigate and prosecute international crimes. Such investigations require substantial financial resources, investigative expertise, and significant legal capacity. Smaller states, lacking these resources, are often unable to effectively participate in the enforcement of universal jurisdiction, even when willing. This disparity highlights the critical role international organizations and donor states play in supporting the capacity building initiatives necessary for the effective implementation of this legal principle. It also underlines the necessity of collaborative efforts to ensure that universal jurisdiction is not merely a theoretical legal concept but a practical tool for accountability. The lack of a truly unified and robust international system for investigating and prosecuting such crimes remains a major challenge to the principle's consistent application.

1.1 Historical Context

The seeds of universal jurisdiction, surprisingly, weren't sown in a grand international treaty or a sweeping declaration. Instead, its roots lie in the murky soil of historical practice, a slow and often uneven growth spurred by egregious violations of human rights and a growing international consensus that some crimes transcend national boundaries. Early instances, often shrouded in the complexities of post-conflict justice and colonial legacies, involved prosecuting pirates and slave traders—individuals whose actions were deemed so heinous they demanded accountability regardless of where they were apprehended. These early applications, though limited in scope and often driven by pragmatic considerations, laid the groundwork for the principle's future expansion. The inconsistent application, however, underscores the inherent difficulties in defining and implementing a concept so inherently challenging to established notions of sovereignty. These early struggles provide invaluable lessons for today's advocates of universal jurisdiction, reminding us that the path towards global criminal accountability is fraught with complexities and compromises.

While the Nuremberg trials following World War II are often cited as a pivotal moment in the development of international criminal law, it's crucial to remember they weren't explicitly based on universal jurisdiction. The Allied powers prosecuted Nazi leaders based on their own military occupation and the unique circumstances of the post-war landscape. However, the Nuremberg principles, particularly regarding the individual criminal responsibility for crimes against humanity, war crimes, and crimes against peace, undeniably influenced subsequent understandings of international criminal law and paved the way for the formalization of universal jurisdiction. This indirect influence is significant; the Nuremberg legacy stands as a testament to the global desire for accountability for the most horrific crimes, even if the legal mechanism employed was not the precise definition of universal jurisdiction we understand today. This legacy continues to shape legal thinking and debates about the scope and application of international criminal justice.

The post-colonial era witnessed a shift. The newly independent nations, grappling with their own histories of oppression and armed conflict, started to see universal jurisdiction not just as a tool for prosecuting their former colonizers but also as a mechanism to hold accountable perpetrators of atrocities within their own borders or beyond. The emergence of international human rights law further contributed to this development, providing a more robust framework for identifying and prosecuting egregious human rights violations. However, the path wasn't simple; many nations, particularly those with strong nationalistic sentiments or those implicated in human rights violations, resisted the principle, asserting it as a threat to their national sovereignty. This conflict between the principle and state sovereignty remains a defining characteristic of the ongoing debate surrounding universal jurisdiction, highlighting the tensions between global justice and national interests.

Consider the Pinochet case in the 1990s. This landmark case, where a former head of state was arrested in Britain on charges of torture, marked a crucial turning point. The Spanish courts' assertion of jurisdiction over Pinochet, a foreign head of state, demonstrated that the concept of universal jurisdiction wasn't merely a theoretical construct but a viable legal tool, capable of reaching even the most powerful individuals. This instance, while controversial and legally complex, showcased the potential and the pitfalls of universal jurisdiction, proving that its application could challenge long-established norms of state immunity and highlight the intricate interaction between national and international legal systems. The case's repercussions extended far beyond the immediate legal proceedings; it triggered an intense international debate on sovereignty, immunity, and the boundaries of national judicial authority.

The historical context of universal jurisdiction isn't merely a matter of tracing its evolution; it's about understanding the political, legal, and ideological forces that have shaped its development. The interplay of various interests—from the victims of human rights abuses to states seeking to uphold their sovereignty—has continuously influenced its application and interpretation. Understanding this historical trajectory is crucial for comprehending the challenges and complexities facing this evolving principle. Without an appreciation of this historical background, the current debates and controversies surrounding universal jurisdiction risk being detached from their historical roots, leading to incomplete and potentially ineffective solutions for ensuring global criminal accountability. The ongoing evolution necessitates a deeper understanding of the path traveled to appreciate the current state of affairs and navigate the road ahead. This necessitates a nuanced approach acknowledging the successes, failures, and enduring tensions shaping the ongoing pursuit of global criminal accountability through universal jurisdiction.

1.2 Early Applications

The concept of universal jurisdiction, though now a cornerstone of international criminal law, had humble beginnings. Early applications, often stemming from individual states' own domestic legal frameworks, lacked the coordinated international approach we see today. These initial forays were characterized by inconsistency, often reflecting the specific political climates and legal interpretations of the time. This lack of harmonization hampered the development of a truly global system for accountability.

Pinpointing the very first instance of what we'd recognize today as universal jurisdiction is difficult. However, certain historical cases serve as important precedents, though their application of universal jurisdiction principles often occurred implicitly, rather than through explicitly stated legal frameworks. Consider, for instance, the trials of pirates – individuals operating outside any clear national jurisdiction, yet subject to prosecution by various maritime powers. While not a fully formed system, these early prosecutions showed a willingness to assert jurisdiction based on the gravity of the crimes committed.

The late 18th and 19th centuries witnessed an evolution in approaches to jurisdiction, with certain states increasingly claiming the right to prosecute individuals for crimes committed abroad, particularly when those crimes violated fundamental norms of international law, like slavery. These cases, while often shrouded in colonial power dynamics, reveal a nascent recognition of a responsibility beyond national borders to address egregious human rights abuses. The inconsistent application, however, highlights the challenges inherent in exercising jurisdiction without a well-defined international legal framework.

Early 20th-century jurisprudence saw little dramatic change in the application of universal jurisdiction. The global political landscape, dominated by state sovereignty concerns, largely inhibited its consistent use. The lack of established international criminal courts or tribunals meant that states' domestic legal systems remained the primary vehicles for holding individuals accountable for international crimes. This reliance on individual state actions, therefore, led to a patchwork of legal approaches, leaving gaps in the system of global criminal accountability.

The post-World War II era marked a significant turning point. The atrocities of the Holocaust and other wartime crimes spurred a growing international consensus on the need for mechanisms to address such grave violations. The Nuremberg and Tokyo trials, while rooted in the victors' justice, laid the groundwork for international criminal law and broadened the scope of international criminal accountability. However, these tribunals were largely ad hoc in nature, created for specific events, rather than representing a fully established system of universal jurisdiction.

The emergence of the International Criminal Court (ICC) in the late 20th and early 21st centuries represents a landmark shift. While not explicitly based on universal jurisdiction in all its applications, the ICC's jurisdiction extends to crimes against humanity, war crimes, and genocide, regardless of where the crimes were committed or the nationality of the perpetrators. The establishment of the ICC significantly advanced the principle of universal jurisdiction by creating a permanent international institution capable of prosecuting such heinous crimes. Even so, the ICC's limitations, including its dependence on state cooperation and its limited prosecutorial capacity, underscore the continued challenges in achieving comprehensive global criminal accountability. It's important to note the various criticisms levelled at the ICC and the continual debate around its effectiveness.

The early applications of universal jurisdiction, though fragmented and often inconsistent, laid the foundation for the international criminal justice system we know today. They demonstrate the gradual evolution of a principle grappling with deeply entrenched ideas of state sovereignty and the inherent difficulties in achieving global cooperation on matters of criminal prosecution. From prosecuting pirates to grappling with the aftermath of genocide, these early cases, however imperfect, highlight humanity's persistent struggle to establish true global accountability for the most serious crimes. The journey from those initial, tentative steps to the complexities of modern universal jurisdiction reveals a continuous, evolving endeavor toward greater justice. The path forward remains challenging but the progress made, however incremental, offers hope for a more just and accountable world. The study of these early applications is crucial in fully understanding the complexities, limitations, and ultimately, the enduring aspiration of universal jurisdiction.

2 Defining Universal Jurisdiction

Universal jurisdiction, a complex legal principle, asserts that certain crimes, so heinous they transcend national boundaries, can be prosecuted in any country regardless of where the crime occurred or the nationality of the perpetrator or victim. Its foundation rests on the idea that some acts are so universally condemned—crimes against humanity, genocide, war crimes, and torture, for example—that their prosecution is a matter of global concern, a responsibility shared by all states. This isn't a new concept; historical examples, though perhaps not explicitly framed as "universal jurisdiction," demonstrate the underlying principle in action. Early instances often involved pirates or slave traders, individuals whose actions defied national borders and whose crimes were deemed so egregious as to warrant punishment wherever they were apprehended.

The legal underpinnings of universal jurisdiction are multifaceted, drawing on customary international law, treaty obligations, and domestic legislation. While no single international treaty comprehensively codifies it, the principle's existence is supported by numerous international legal instruments and judicial decisions. Key principles include the concept of aut dedere aut judicare ("to extradite or to prosecute"), obligating states either to extradite suspects to a state with jurisdiction or to prosecute them themselves. Furthermore, the principle of jus cogens, referring to peremptory norms of international law, reinforces the notion that certain fundamental principles, such as the prohibition against genocide, are binding on all states irrespective of any contrary domestic law. The interpretation and application of these principles, however, remain a subject of ongoing debate and judicial interpretation, leading to inconsistencies in practice.

Defining the crimes covered under universal jurisdiction is crucial. While the core crimes generally accepted are genocide, crimes against humanity, war crimes, and torture, the precise scope can differ based on national laws and international court interpretations. Furthermore, the threshold for proving jurisdiction can be high, requiring a strong evidentiary basis demonstrating the alleged crime's severity and the perpetrator's culpability. There's often a tension between the broad aspirational goal of holding perpetrators accountable for egregious crimes and the practical realities of prosecuting complex cases involving multiple jurisdictions, witnesses, and evidentiary challenges. The legal standard for determining guilt remains a cornerstone of the system, and the varying legal systems' capacity to meet that standard adds to its overall complexity.

The practical challenges in applying universal jurisdiction are significant. States are often hesitant to exercise it due to concerns about state sovereignty and potential diplomatic repercussions. Some view it as an encroachment on national autonomy, preferring to prioritize their own national interests over global justice. Even if a state is willing to prosecute, considerable resources are needed: specialized investigators, interpreters, legal expertise, and secure detention facilities. International cooperation is also paramount, yet achieving this cooperation—for example, in securing evidence or witness testimony across borders—can be difficult. The lack of a centralized international body to coordinate and support prosecutions further hampers the effective use of universal jurisdiction. The scarcity of resources coupled with the logistical issues involved in international judicial cooperation, ultimately limits the application of the principle.

Political obstacles further impede the application of universal jurisdiction. Governments may prioritize diplomatic relations over the pursuit of justice, potentially refusing to prosecute individuals accused of serious international

crimes if it risks damaging their relationship with another country. Furthermore, some states may lack the political will to take on the considerable logistical and financial burdens associated with these complex prosecutions, leading to a lack of action on cases where the individual is within their legal power to prosecute. This reticence, despite the legal mandate, often undermines the very principle's effectiveness in preventing impunity.
The impact of universal jurisdiction on international law remains a subject of ongoing debate. While its application has been instrumental in holding individuals accountable for serious international crimes, its sporadic and inconsistent application raises questions about its overall effectiveness. The number of successful prosecutions remains relatively low, compared to the scale of atrocities committed globally. This does not diminish its importance as a legal principle and moral imperative, but highlights the substantial challenges involved in its implementation and the critical need for reform. The future efficacy of the principle requires a multifaceted approach involving legal harmonization, increased international cooperation, and greater resource allocation. Ultimately, the pursuit of global criminal accountability through universal jurisdiction remains a challenging yet crucial aspect of international law. Its continued evolution is essential in addressing impunity and promoting justice on a global scale.

2.1 Legal Foundations

The bedrock of universal jurisdiction rests on a complex interplay of customary international law, treaty obligations, and evolving state practice. While no single, universally ratified treaty explicitly codifies universal jurisdiction in its entirety, its existence is supported by a confluence of legal instruments and judicial pronouncements. The principle emerges from the recognition that certain crimes, so heinous and egregious in their violation of fundamental human rights, transcend national boundaries, demanding accountability regardless of where the crime occurred or the nationality of the perpetrator. This understanding is deeply rooted in the concept of jus cogens, compelling norms of international law that cannot be derogated from. These norms, reflecting the collective conscience of humanity, dictate that certain acts, such as genocide, crimes against humanity, war crimes, and torture, are so fundamental in their violation of human dignity that all states have a responsibility to prosecute the perpetrators, regardless of their connection to the state itself. This inherent responsibility is the foundational legal basis for universal jurisdiction, albeit one subject to ongoing debate and refinement.

This principle's legal legitimacy stems from several sources. The International Criminal Court (ICC) Statute, though not directly establishing universal jurisdiction as its primary basis, implicitly acknowledges its existence through its complementarity principle. This principle allows national courts to retain primary jurisdiction over crimes covered by the ICC Statute, provided that they are genuinely investigating and prosecuting them. Therefore, the existence of a robust domestic system of universal jurisdiction actually enhances the effectiveness of the ICC. Furthermore, numerous national legal systems incorporate provisions allowing their courts to exercise jurisdiction over certain international crimes, reflecting the growing recognition of universal jurisdiction as a legitimate principle of international law. These national laws, however diverse in their specific provisions, demonstrate a pattern of legal acceptance of this doctrine, thereby reinforcing its customary international law status. Such legal acceptance has often been spurred by high-profile cases where national courts have prosecuted individuals for atrocities committed far beyond their national territory.

However, the application of universal jurisdiction isn't without its constraints. The principle is often subject to interpretative complexities and challenges. Determining the precise threshold for exercising jurisdiction—the point where a crime is sufficiently grave to trigger universal jurisdiction— remains a subject of ongoing debate. Some argue for a more restrictive approach, emphasizing the need for a clear link between the crime and the forum state, while others advocate for a broader interpretation, prioritizing the severity of the crime itself. This tension between the gravity of the offense and the connection to the forum state is central to the ongoing legal discourse surrounding universal jurisdiction. This necessitates careful consideration of the specific circumstances of each case, weighing competing arguments concerning state sovereignty, the potential for political manipulation, and the practical limitations of enforcement. The lack of a universally agreed-upon definition of "grave breaches" frequently leads to inconsistencies in application across different legal systems. Adding further complexity are questions surrounding the admissibility of evidence obtained outside the forum state's jurisdiction, the application of different legal standards, and ensuring fairness in proceedings. International cooperation, crucial for effective prosecution, frequently faces difficulties due to varying national interests and legal frameworks.

Despite the challenges, the legal foundations of universal jurisdiction remain robust. The principle continues to evolve, shaped by judicial decisions, state practice, and ongoing academic discourse. Its significance lies not merely in its theoretical existence but in its practical application. The ongoing prosecutions under universal jurisdiction demonstrate its capacity to hold individuals accountable for the most serious international crimes, affirming the global commitment to justice and the imperative to prevent impunity. The future direction of universal jurisdiction will likely depend on a more comprehensive and coherent international framework, potentially through treaty codification or a strengthening of international cooperation mechanisms. This would ensure greater consistency and predictability in its application, contributing to a more robust system of global criminal accountability. The ultimate aim, undeniably, is to strengthen the rule of law in the international arena, deterring future atrocities and ensuring justice for victims. However, navigating the delicate balance between state sovereignty and the pursuit of justice remains a fundamental and ongoing challenge. The legal framework must evolve to address this critical balance, ensuring both effectiveness and fairness in its application.

2.2 Jurisdictional Principles

Understanding the jurisdictional principles underpinning universal jurisdiction is crucial. It's not a simple matter of arresting anyone, anywhere, for any crime. Rather, it's a complex legal framework built upon specific, well-defined principles that aim to balance the pursuit of justice with the sovereign rights of nations. The application of universal jurisdiction hinges on the nature of the crime, the perpetrator's presence within the prosecuting state's territory, and the absence of any compelling reason to defer jurisdiction to another state better positioned to prosecute. This chapter will unpack these intricate elements.

The most fundamental principle is the concept of aut dedere aut judicare, often translated as "to extradite or to prosecute." This principle, enshrined in numerous international legal instruments and customary international law, imposes an obligation on states to either extradite an alleged perpetrator of certain crimes to a state with jurisdiction or to prosecute them within their own courts. This principle directly addresses the issue of jurisdictional gaps that often arise in cases of international crimes, ensuring that perpetrators are not left unpunished simply due to the lack of a readily available prosecuting jurisdiction. It's a pivotal principle, forcing states to actively engage with international criminal accountability.

However, aut dedere aut judicare is not without its complexities. States are not obligated to prosecute unless they have sufficient grounds to do so. This consideration is particularly relevant in instances where a state lacks the resources or expertise to conduct a fair and effective trial. The principle does not automatically grant jurisdiction to every state; rather, it establishes an obligation to take action, the nature of which will depend on the state's specific circumstances and capabilities. The principle also acknowledges the need for states to consider the potential for abuse and political manipulation in the application of universal jurisdiction.

The principle of passive personality grants a state jurisdiction over crimes committed against its nationals, regardless of where the crime occurred. This principle's application in the context of universal jurisdiction is often debated, with some arguing that it should be limited to specific heinous crimes against humanity, genocide, or war crimes, and others advocating for broader application. However, the invocation of passive personality must be carefully considered to avoid conflicts with the territorial sovereignty of other states and to prevent the abuse of jurisdiction for politically motivated prosecutions. The application needs to be measured, balanced, and demonstrably not designed for malicious purposes.

Another relevant principle is that of protective jurisdiction, which allows a state to assert jurisdiction over acts committed abroad that threaten its national security or vital interests. While this principle finds its basis in the need to protect a state's essential functions, its application requires a careful assessment of proportionality and the potential for conflicts with other jurisdictional principles. Overly broad interpretations could lead to the extraterritorial reach of a state's criminal law, potentially undermining the principle of state sovereignty and contributing to international tensions. It's a powerful tool, but one that must be wielded with precision and restraint.

Finally, the principle of universality itself is a cornerstone of universal jurisdiction. It recognizes the inherent gravity of certain crimes against humanity, genocide, war crimes, and torture as crimes that transcend national borders and affect the interests of the entire international community. The principle establishes that states have a right and, in many cases, a duty to prosecute individuals for these grave crimes regardless of where the crimes were committed or the nationality of the perpetrators or victims. This principle highlights the international community's shared responsibility to address impunity for the most heinous crimes.

In conclusion, the jurisdictional principles governing universal jurisdiction are not monolithic. They are multifaceted and require careful consideration. Their application should always be guided by considerations of fairness, proportionality, and the overall objective of preventing impunity for serious international crimes. Balancing these competing interests requires a sophisticated understanding of international law and a nuanced appreciation of the political realities influencing international criminal justice. The effective and responsible application of universal jurisdiction hinges on striking this balance. Furthermore, the principles themselves are constantly evolving, shaped by the experience of numerous prosecutions, judicial interpretations, and the evolving norms of international law.

2.3 Crimes Covered

The core of universal jurisdiction lies in its ability to prosecute individuals for the gravest crimes, regardless of where the offenses occurred or the nationality of the perpetrator or victim. This principle, grounded in the idea of jus cogens norms – peremptory norms of international law that cannot be violated – allows states to claim jurisdiction over crimes that outrage the conscience of humanity. These crimes are not merely violations of domestic law, but profound assaults on the international legal order itself. They are crimes against all of humankind, deserving of universal condemnation and punishment. The very nature of these crimes demands a global response, transcending national boundaries and the limitations of conventional jurisdictional approaches. Their scale and impact necessitate a mechanism for accountability that is not contingent on the cooperation of the state where the crime took place, or the nationality of the alleged perpetrator. This is precisely the role universal jurisdiction plays, offering a crucial avenue for justice in situations where national courts may be unwilling or unable to act.

Crimes covered under universal jurisdiction are typically defined by international treaties and customary international law. Crimes against humanity, genocide, war crimes, and torture are commonly cited examples. Each of these categories encompasses a wide range of specific acts, making precise definition crucial. For instance, genocide, as defined by the 1948 Genocide Convention, involves acts committed with intent to destroy, in whole or in part, a national, ethnical, racial or religious group. Similarly, crimes against humanity involve widespread or systematic attacks against any civilian population. War crimes are serious violations of the laws of war, such as the deliberate targeting of civilians or the use of prohibited weapons. Torture, involving the intentional infliction of severe pain or suffering for purposes such as obtaining information or punishment, is also a crime universally condemned and subject to prosecution under this principle.

However, it's vital to acknowledge the complexities and nuances involved in defining these crimes. The precise parameters of each category have been the subject of considerable debate and judicial interpretation. What constitutes "widespread" or "systematic" attacks for crimes against humanity? What level of intent is necessary to establish genocide? These are questions that have been addressed by international courts and tribunals, but they continue to present challenges in practice. The evolving nature of international law and the increasing complexity of armed conflict contribute to ongoing debates about the precise scope and application of universal jurisdiction to these atrocities. The interpretation of these crimes is not static and evolves based on judicial precedents, treaty development, and the broader understanding of human rights.

Furthermore, the list of crimes covered by universal jurisdiction is not exhaustive. There is a growing movement to include other serious violations of international law, such as piracy, terrorism and certain forms of environmental crimes. This expansion reflects both the increasing recognition of the transnational nature of crime and the need for robust international mechanisms to address increasingly complex global challenges. The inclusion of additional crimes would necessitate a careful consideration of their severity, their transnational nature, and the existing international legal framework, ensuring a balanced approach that avoids stretching the principle beyond its intended purpose. Each expansion must be carefully considered and debated in the international legal community to safeguard the principle's integrity and effectiveness.

Ultimately, the application of universal jurisdiction hinges on a delicate balance between promoting accountability for the most serious crimes and respecting the principles of state sovereignty. While universal jurisdiction serves as a critical tool for addressing impunity, the practical challenges of its implementation are significant. This includes obtaining evidence across borders, securing the cooperation of other states, and overcoming political obstacles. The effectiveness of universal jurisdiction is not simply a matter of legal doctrine but also a function of political will, international cooperation, and the resources available to pursue these complex cases. The future of universal jurisdiction depends on the continued development of international law, strengthening of international cooperation, and the unwavering commitment to the pursuit of justice for the victims of egregious human rights violations.

3 Scope and Limitations

State sovereignty remains a cornerstone of international law, often clashing directly with the expansive reach of universal jurisdiction. The principle, while powerful in its potential to hold perpetrators of heinous crimes accountable, must navigate the delicate balance of national interests and international justice. A nation's right to govern itself and its citizens is paramount, creating inherent limitations on the ability of other states to assert jurisdiction over crimes committed outside their territory. This inherent tension necessitates careful consideration of the potential for friction and the need for robust mechanisms to prevent unilateral actions from undermining international stability. Such considerations are not merely academic exercises; they represent critical hurdles in the practical application of universal jurisdiction.

The practical challenges are numerous and often interconnected. Securing the arrest and extradition of suspects, for instance, demands cooperation from states that may be reluctant to relinquish individuals within their borders, particularly if those individuals are high-ranking officials or possess significant political influence. Evidence gathering in international settings frequently presents logistical and jurisdictional complexities. Obtaining testimony from witnesses scattered across different countries often involves navigating conflicting legal systems, language barriers, and resource limitations. Moreover, the cost of conducting protracted international investigations and prosecutions, involving expert witnesses, translators, and legal teams, can be prohibitive, particularly for states with limited resources.

These financial burdens can significantly hamper the effective application of universal jurisdiction, limiting its reach and impact.
Navigating legal intricacies further complicates the process. Differing legal systems and interpretations of international law can lead to conflicting judgments and disagreements over jurisdictional claims. The precise definition of crimes under universal jurisdiction and the circumstances under which it can be legitimately invoked remains a subject of ongoing debate, generating inconsistencies across various jurisdictions. The threshold for establishing a credible link between the crime and a particular state, for instance, can be difficult to prove, leaving room for legal maneuvering and challenges. This uncertainty underlines the necessity for greater clarity and harmonization of legal frameworks to enhance the predictability and effectiveness of universal jurisdiction.
Political considerations frequently overshadow the legal merits of universal jurisdiction. States might hesitate to prosecute individuals if doing so could jeopardize delicate diplomatic relationships or lead to negative political repercussions. Domestic political pressures can also influence decisions regarding prosecution, particularly when powerful vested interests are involved. The inherent political sensitivity associated with prosecuting internationally recognized figures adds another layer of complexity. International consensus regarding the application of universal jurisdiction is still far from complete, with varying levels of support and commitment from different states. This uneven landscape limits the collective strength and consistent enforcement of the principle.
The lack of adequate judicial capacity further restricts the operational effectiveness of universal jurisdiction. Many states lack the necessary legal expertise, infrastructure, and resources to handle complex international criminal cases. Training judges, prosecutors, and investigators in the intricacies of international criminal law is crucial but resource-intensive. Adequate infrastructure for securing evidence, managing cross-border cooperation, and providing fair trials for defendants must also be developed. The absence of these essential elements severely undermines the capacity

of states to effectively utilize universal jurisdiction. Moreover, the absence of sufficient resources often limits the ability to pursue complex cases that require extensive investigation and prolonged court proceedings, hindering the application of universal jurisdiction.

Resource constraints are not just financial; they also extend to the availability of trained personnel. Specialized skills are needed in international law, evidence gathering, forensic analysis, and expert testimony. Developing and retaining these skilled professionals demands long-term investment in training and capacity-building. International cooperation is crucial but often hindered by practical obstacles. States may be unwilling to share sensitive information or extradite suspects if they fear the legal processes in other jurisdictions will be inadequate or politically motivated. A lack of trust and the absence of agreed-upon mechanisms for collaboration continue to obstruct effective international cooperation in the application of universal jurisdiction. The establishment of clear guidelines and protocols to guide cooperation would be a beneficial step to alleviate these limitations.

In summary, while universal jurisdiction offers a vital tool for holding perpetrators of grave international crimes accountable, its implementation faces significant scope and limitations. These constraints stem from the inherent tension between state sovereignty and international justice, as well as from practical challenges in securing cooperation, gathering evidence, securing resources, and navigating complex legal frameworks. Overcoming these obstacles requires a concerted global effort to strengthen international cooperation, improve judicial capacity, and clarify the legal standards governing the application of universal jurisdiction. Only through such efforts can the principle's considerable potential for promoting global criminal accountability be fully realized.

3.1 State Sovereignty

State sovereignty, a cornerstone of international relations, presents a significant hurdle to the effective implementation of universal jurisdiction. The principle of non-intervention in the domestic affairs of other states, deeply ingrained in international law, often clashes with the assertion of jurisdiction by a state over crimes committed elsewhere. This inherent tension creates a complex interplay between the desire for global criminal accountability and the respect for national autonomy, frequently resulting in political friction and legal challenges. The delicate balance required necessitates a nuanced understanding of both principles.

Many states, particularly those with strong nationalistic sentiments or a history of resisting external interference, view universal jurisdiction with considerable suspicion. They perceive it as a potential infringement on their sovereignty, arguing that it undermines their exclusive right to prosecute crimes committed within their borders. This perspective is often fueled by concerns about political motivations behind the exercise of universal jurisdiction, potentially leading to accusations of selective justice or attempts to exert undue influence on other nations. These concerns, whether valid or perceived, can lead to significant diplomatic obstacles and hinder cooperation with investigations and prosecutions. The delicate dance between sovereign equality and the pursuit of justice for international crimes presents a major challenge for the international community.

Furthermore, the practical application of universal jurisdiction frequently encounters limitations rooted in the principle of state sovereignty. The extradition of suspects, a crucial element in bringing perpetrators to justice, often hinges on the willingness of the state where the suspect resides to cooperate. Even in the absence of explicit opposition, bureaucratic hurdles and legal processes can delay or even prevent extradition, highlighting the power states retain over their own territories and citizens. This jurisdictional complexity is often compounded by the lack of universally recognized standards for defining and prosecuting certain international crimes, leading to discrepancies in legal interpretations and further impeding cooperation. States may decline to extradite based on national interpretations of laws or perceived violations of their own sovereignty.

The tension between universal jurisdiction and state sovereignty isn't merely theoretical; it manifests in concrete ways. Consider the difficulties in securing the cooperation of states with weak or failing judicial systems. In such environments, the pursuit of universal jurisdiction can be viewed not as a means of justice but as an intrusion into internal affairs, exacerbating already fragile political situations. The fear of interference, whether justified or not, can fuel opposition and render even well-intentioned attempts at prosecution unproductive. This inherent sensitivity underscores the need for careful diplomacy and a deep understanding of the political realities within each state involved. International cooperation requires not only legal frameworks but also political will, and that will is often tested when state sovereignty is seemingly compromised.

Addressing this challenge necessitates a multi-faceted approach. Firstly, a stronger emphasis on building trust and fostering collaboration between states is critical. This involves facilitating dialogues, promoting mutual respect for national legal systems, and recognizing the legitimate concerns about sovereignty. Secondly, developing clear and universally accepted standards for the prosecution of international crimes can help to mitigate potential disagreements over jurisdiction. This would involve standardizing legal definitions, procedures, and evidence admissibility across jurisdictions, thereby reducing ambiguity and increasing the likelihood of cooperation. Finally, providing technical and financial assistance to states with weaker judicial systems can enhance their capacity to handle international crimes themselves, reducing the reliance on external interventions and respecting the principle of state sovereignty. The goal isn't to eliminate state sovereignty but to create a system where justice and sovereignty are compatible objectives.

3.2 Practical Challenges

The practical application of universal jurisdiction faces significant hurdles. Navigating these complexities requires careful consideration of several key factors. Resource constraints, for instance, are a considerable obstacle for many states, particularly those with already overburdened judicial systems.

Prosecutions under universal jurisdiction are often lengthy, complex and demanding, requiring specialized expertise, extensive investigations, and significant financial resources which many nations lack. This financial burden can deter states from taking on such cases, even when they have the legal authority to do so. The sheer logistical challenges involved in gathering evidence across international borders, securing witness testimony, and overcoming language barriers add further weight to the resource burden. Successfully prosecuting cases under universal jurisdiction demands significant financial investments in training, technology, and support staff, all further straining limited resources.

Beyond resource limitations, securing international cooperation presents another critical challenge. Universal jurisdiction often necessitates collaboration between states, involving the extradition of suspects, the sharing of evidence, and mutual legal assistance. However, political considerations, differing legal systems, and a lack of trust can significantly impede this crucial cooperation. Some states may be reluctant to cooperate if they fear that doing so could set a precedent that might be used against them in the future. Others might lack the legal mechanisms or political will to assist in foreign prosecutions, even when legally obligated. The absence of a universally accepted mechanism for ensuring cooperation significantly hampers the effectiveness of universal jurisdiction.

The political landscape also creates considerable obstacles. States may be hesitant to assert universal jurisdiction, particularly when it involves powerful individuals or countries. Political pressure, diplomatic sensitivities, and fears of retaliatory actions can dissuade states from prosecuting cases that may have international repercussions. The potential for strained relations with other states adds a significant political cost that often outweighs the perceived benefits of prosecution. This political sensitivity often results in a cautious approach to invoking universal jurisdiction, prioritizing national interests over international justice. Consequently, cases that could significantly advance the cause of universal jurisdiction often go unprosecuted due to political considerations.

Judicial capacity poses yet another substantial challenge. The complexity of international crimes necessitates judges and prosecutors with specialized knowledge and experience in international law, human rights law, and criminal procedure. Not all states possess this level of judicial expertise, leading to potential inconsistencies in the application of universal jurisdiction and the risk of flawed prosecutions. Furthermore, the specialized nature of these cases requires significant training for judges and prosecutors, which can be costly and time-consuming. Moreover, there is a continuing need for enhancing training programs focusing on the specific complexities of universal jurisdiction, including evidentiary standards, procedural requirements, and legal interpretations of the crimes under scrutiny. This lack of capacity impacts the quality and consistency of prosecutions under universal jurisdiction.

Moreover, the issue of potential abuse of universal jurisdiction adds to the complexity. Some argue that it could be used as a tool for political vendettas or for targeting individuals based on political or ideological motivations rather than on the merits of the case. The potential for selective prosecution and the possibility of biased or unfair trials significantly undermine the legitimacy and effectiveness of universal jurisdiction. This necessitates clear guidelines and safeguards to prevent the abuse of this principle. Moreover, international mechanisms are needed to ensure accountability and transparency in the exercise of universal jurisdiction, promoting fairness and trust.

Finally, there's the challenge of defining the scope of universal jurisdiction. The line between legitimate exercises of this principle and violations of state sovereignty remains a subject of ongoing debate. Finding a balance between upholding the principle of universal jurisdiction and respecting the sovereignty of states is crucial for its long-term success. This requires a nuanced and context-specific approach, with careful consideration of both legal and political ramifications. International cooperation and dialogue are critical in achieving this balance, ensuring that the application of universal jurisdiction is both effective and respects the principles of international law.

Clearer guidelines and better mechanisms for determining the appropriateness of invoking universal jurisdiction in individual cases are essential to address this challenge.

4 Challenges to Implementation

Political will, or rather, the lack thereof, frequently presents a formidable barrier. Governments, often swayed by domestic political considerations or strategic alliances, may hesitate to prosecute individuals accused of international crimes, even if evidence is compelling. This reluctance stems from a variety of sources: fear of jeopardizing relations with other states, concerns about the potential for retaliatory actions, and the inherent complexities of navigating the delicate balance between national interests and international obligations. Such political calculations often outweigh the imperative of upholding justice, leading to inaction or even outright obstruction. The absence of consistent and robust political support internationally hinders the effectiveness of universal jurisdiction mechanisms significantly. It is a challenge that requires concerted diplomatic efforts and a global shift in prioritization towards justice over political expediency.

Enforcement difficulties are equally daunting. Even when a state asserts jurisdiction, actually apprehending and bringing a suspect to trial presents numerous logistical and practical hurdles. Individuals accused of atrocities may be located in countries unwilling to cooperate or lack the resources to assist in extradition. They may enjoy protection from powerful entities, rendering efforts to secure their arrest near impossible. Furthermore, the process of gathering evidence across borders, often involving multiple jurisdictions and languages, demands extensive resources and sophisticated investigative skills. The sheer complexity, time, and costs associated with international investigations can overwhelm even the most well-resourced national systems. Successful prosecution necessitates not only legal frameworks but also robust enforcement capabilities that are adequately supported and coordinated.

Resource limitations pose a significant constraint. Investigating and prosecuting international crimes is a costly and time-consuming undertaking. It demands specialized expertise in international law, forensic science, and investigative techniques. States with limited financial resources often lack the capacity to build the necessary infrastructure or train personnel capable of handling these complex cases. This disparity in resources creates an uneven playing field, favoring states with more substantial financial capabilities to pursue justice effectively. The absence of substantial international funding for supporting states in these endeavors further exacerbates this imbalance. A robust mechanism for equitable resource distribution is crucial to ensure that universal jurisdiction is not a privilege of the wealthy but a right available to all victims.

The lack of international cooperation is a major impediment. Effective prosecution of international crimes often requires the collaboration of multiple states, sharing evidence, expertise, and resources. However, states may be reluctant to cooperate due to political sensitivities, competing national interests, or a lack of trust. Concerns about sovereignty or potential legal repercussions within their own jurisdictions can inhibit the sharing of crucial information and witness testimony. The absence of consistent and reliable mechanisms for international cooperation hampers efforts to build strong cases and bring perpetrators to justice. This necessitates the development of clear and legally binding international agreements promoting cooperation and mutual assistance.

Judicial capacity presents another considerable challenge. National judiciaries may lack the expertise, experience, and resources needed to handle complex cases involving international law. Specialized training and capacity-building initiatives are necessary to equip judges and prosecutors with the knowledge and skills required to effectively navigate the legal intricacies inherent in these prosecutions. Moreover, the sheer volume of evidence gathered in such cases often necessitates innovative approaches to managing and analyzing information. The creation of specialized international courts or tribunals may provide an alternative route, ensuring adequate judicial capacity and expertise is available. Yet, even in such specialized courts, securing consistent cooperation and access to witnesses and evidence across international borders remains paramount.

4.1 Political Obstacles

Political maneuvering often undermines the application of universal jurisdiction. States, particularly those implicated in or allied with alleged perpetrators, may exert considerable pressure on other nations to refrain from pursuing investigations or prosecutions. This pressure can take many forms, from diplomatic protests and threats to economic sanctions or the withdrawal of aid. Such actions directly contradict the very principle of universal jurisdiction, which is intended to transcend national interests and prioritize the accountability of perpetrators of egregious crimes. The interplay of national interests and the pursuit of global justice forms a complex dynamic that frequently stymies the effective implementation of universal jurisdiction, forcing a delicate balancing act.

National security concerns frequently serve as a justification for opposing universal jurisdiction. Governments may argue that investigations into alleged crimes, especially those involving past events or high-ranking officials, could compromise sensitive intelligence operations or ongoing diplomatic relations. This argument, while seemingly plausible in certain contexts, can be manipulated to shield perpetrators from accountability. The fear of jeopardizing national security often becomes a political shield, protecting those who might otherwise be held responsible for grave violations of international law; a strategy that undermines the foundation of international justice.

Furthermore, domestic political considerations play a significant role. Governments may face domestic pressure from various actors— including political parties, lobbying groups, or even public opinion— to avoid actions that might be perceived as harming national interests, even if it means undermining the enforcement of international justice. This domestic political landscape can be particularly challenging for states considering investigations or prosecutions that could create diplomatic tensions with powerful allies or adversaries, leading to self-censorship to avoid potential backlash from their own populations, ultimately diminishing the effectiveness of universal jurisdiction.

The selective application of universal jurisdiction is another major obstacle. While the principle ostensibly applies universally, its implementation is often far from uniform. Powerful states may be more likely to face scrutiny than weaker ones, creating a perception of bias and undermining the principle's credibility. This uneven application raises concerns about the fairness and consistency of the system, potentially exacerbating existing power imbalances in the international arena. The selective nature of its application can weaken the global legitimacy and impact of universal jurisdiction.

Finally, a lack of political will among states poses a significant impediment to the effective use of universal jurisdiction. Even when there is a legal basis for prosecution, a lack of political commitment can result in inaction. States might hesitate to initiate investigations or prosecutions due to concerns about diplomatic fallout, financial costs, or simply a lack of priority given to international justice over domestic affairs. This lack of political will hampers the development and effectiveness of universal jurisdiction, highlighting its critical dependence on global cooperation and willingness to prioritize accountability for serious crimes. Without robust political will among nation-states, the mechanisms designed for enforcing universal jurisdiction risk becoming ineffective tools for global criminal accountability.

4.2 Enforcement Difficulties

Securing convictions under universal jurisdiction presents formidable challenges. The sheer complexity of navigating multiple legal systems, often with conflicting priorities and interpretations of international law, creates significant hurdles. Investigating crimes committed across borders necessitates international collaboration, a process often hampered by political sensitivities, bureaucratic inertia, and the reluctance of states to surrender their citizens. Furthermore, securing the extradition of suspects is frequently a protracted and difficult affair, hindered by legal technicalities, political pressure, and the lack of robust extradition treaties covering all relevant crimes. Success requires meticulous planning, resource-intensive investigations, and a high burden of proof to overcome inherent jurisdictional uncertainties.

Evidence gathering poses a particularly acute problem. Crimes under universal jurisdiction often occur in remote locations, with witnesses scattered across multiple jurisdictions. Gathering and verifying evidence, especially in the face of state non-cooperation or active obstruction, demands extensive resources, specialized expertise, and significant time commitments. Furthermore, language barriers, cultural differences, and differing legal frameworks further complicate the process, often delaying or preventing the effective presentation of evidence in court. This can significantly weaken the prosecution's case and reduce the likelihood of a successful conviction.

The availability of resources directly correlates with the efficacy of universal jurisdiction. Many states, especially those with limited budgets or those not directly affected by the crimes under investigation, lack the financial and human resources to effectively pursue complex international criminal cases. Consequently, investigations may be inadequately funded, leading to limited investigative capacity and potentially missed opportunities to gather crucial evidence. Likewise, a lack of specialized personnel, such as linguists, forensic experts, and legal professionals with expertise in international law, further compounds the problem, potentially hindering investigations and prosecutions. Without adequate resources, securing justice becomes a monumental, often insurmountable task.

Political considerations frequently impede effective enforcement. States are often reluctant to investigate or prosecute cases that could damage their

diplomatic relations or upset powerful interests, even when strong evidence suggests guilt. Concerns about national sovereignty, even in cases of egregious human rights violations, can lead to political pressure to avoid prosecuting suspects, resulting in the triumph of political expediency over the pursuit of justice. This compromises the credibility and effectiveness of universal jurisdiction. Likewise, states may be unwilling to cooperate in investigations or extraditions for fear of damaging diplomatic relations or economic partnerships, hindering efforts to bring perpetrators to account.
Furthermore, the judicial capacity to handle complex international criminal cases often proves inadequate. Even if a state possesses the political will and resources to pursue a case, its judicial system may lack the experience, expertise, or institutional framework necessary to effectively manage complex international trials. The legal and procedural intricacies involved in cases under universal jurisdiction demand a high degree of legal and technical sophistication, exceeding the capabilities of many judicial systems. This lack of capacity can lead to delays, procedural errors, and ultimately, a failure to secure convictions. Consequently, the effectiveness of the legal system in dispensing justice is undermined, regardless of resources and evidence. Justice, then, is rarely truly served when a trial is rendered ineffective by a judiciary not up to the task.
Finally, the lack of consistent international cooperation further undermines enforcement. Effective application of universal jurisdiction relies heavily on international cooperation among states in areas like investigation, evidence gathering, witness protection, and extradition. The absence of a global enforcement mechanism or a uniform approach to cooperation often leads to fragmented, uncoordinated efforts, allowing perpetrators to escape justice. The lack of universally accepted standards and procedures for international investigations, prosecutions, and extraditions can further exacerbate this problem. Consequently, without a coordinated international approach, the effectiveness of universal jurisdiction is severely hampered, leaving many perpetrators unpunished.

4.3 Resource Constraints

Resource limitations pose a significant, arguably the most significant, hurdle to the effective implementation of universal jurisdiction. The sheer cost of investigating, prosecuting, and incarcerating individuals accused of international crimes is substantial. These costs encompass everything from travel expenses for investigators and witnesses to the provision of legal representation for both the accused and victims, often requiring multilingual capabilities and expert testimony across numerous jurisdictions. Furthermore, securing and safeguarding evidence collected internationally can be extremely expensive and logistically challenging, requiring specialist skills and cross-border cooperation. The need for secure detention facilities, often with specialized medical and security provisions for high-profile detainees, further exacerbates financial burdens, potentially exceeding the budgetary capabilities of many states willing to pursue such cases.

Often overlooked is the human cost associated with resource constraints. Overworked and under-resourced investigators and prosecutors face immense pressure to deliver results within limited budgets. This inevitably leads to compromises, often impacting the quality of investigations and the thoroughness of prosecutions. A lack of sufficient resources also creates a bottleneck effect: cases are delayed or even abandoned, allowing perpetrators to evade justice. This lack of prompt and efficient processing sends a dangerous message—that impunity is a viable option, undermining the very purpose of universal jurisdiction. The emotional toll on those involved in these complex and often emotionally draining cases, coupled with inadequate support systems, should not be underestimated. It's a critical element often missed in the broader analysis of the challenges of implementing universal jurisdiction.

Beyond financial and human resources, technological limitations also play a critical role. Accessing and analyzing complex digital evidence often requires specialized software and expert personnel, representing a considerable investment. The digital footprint of modern crimes often extends across national borders, complicating evidence gathering and requiring sophisticated forensic capabilities. The constant evolution of technology means that institutions need to maintain their technological edge, leading to ongoing and substantial costs for training and equipment upgrades. Furthermore, the need for secure digital communication channels and platforms to facilitate international cooperation in investigations adds another layer of complexity and cost. Without adequate technological infrastructure and expertise, the effectiveness of investigations and prosecutions can be severely compromised, rendering justice unattainable.

The consequences of these resource constraints extend far beyond individual cases. They contribute to a wider perception of injustice and erode public confidence in the international legal system. When resources are scarce, prosecutions are selective and inconsistent. This perceived bias, even if unintentional, can fuel resentment and mistrust, undermining the legitimacy and effectiveness of the principle of universal jurisdiction as a whole. Critically, it can discourage states from assuming the responsibilities inherent in enforcing universal jurisdiction, further perpetuating the cycle of impunity. A robust system requires consistent, well-funded investment, a reality far from the present circumstances for many states engaging with this complex legal principle.

Therefore, addressing resource constraints is not merely a logistical matter; it is fundamentally crucial for the success of universal jurisdiction. Without significant and sustained investment in human, technological, and financial resources, the goal of global criminal accountability remains a distant prospect. This requires a collective effort from states, international organizations, and civil society to find innovative and sustainable solutions. This might involve mechanisms for shared funding, capacity-building programs, and technical assistance initiatives to ensure a more equitable and effective distribution of resources. Ultimately, a commitment to alleviating these constraints is indispensable for the future of universal jurisdiction and its crucial role in upholding international law and accountability. Only then will the goal of global criminal accountability become less of a grand pursuit and more of a realized reality.

4.4 Lack of Cooperation

International cooperation, the lifeblood of effective universal jurisdiction, frequently falters. This lack of cooperation manifests in various frustrating ways, hindering the pursuit of justice for heinous international crimes. States often prioritize national interests, even when confronted with overwhelming evidence of atrocities committed beyond their borders. Reluctance to share information, extradite suspects, or even acknowledge the legitimacy of universal jurisdiction itself, creates significant roadblocks. This isn't solely a matter of malevolence; resource constraints, differing legal systems, and political sensitivities all play a role. The result, however, remains the same: impunity for perpetrators and a weakening of the international legal order.

The absence of robust cooperation mechanisms severely limits the effectiveness of universal jurisdiction. International treaties and agreements exist, aiming to facilitate cooperation, but their implementation is often inconsistent and dependent on individual state will. The absence of a truly global enforcement body capable of compelling states to cooperate creates a power imbalance, allowing states to shield individuals accused of grave crimes from justice based on their own national self-interest. This selective application of international norms undermines the very principle of universal jurisdiction, transforming it from a powerful tool for accountability into a less reliable instrument for justice.

Consider the practical implications. A state might possess crucial evidence regarding a suspect but refuse to share it, citing national security concerns or the lack of a bilateral extradition treaty. Prosecutors in states attempting to apply universal jurisdiction are left handicapped, struggling to build a solid case. Even when extradition is granted, delays can be crippling, allowing suspects to evade justice or crucial evidence to deteriorate. The bureaucratic hurdles and often opaque processes involved in international legal cooperation can further obstruct the timely pursuit of justice. These complexities disproportionately affect smaller states or those lacking sufficient resources to navigate the intricate web of international legal procedures.

Beyond the formal legal obstacles, informal barriers are equally formidable. Diplomatic pressure, political considerations, and the fear of jeopardizing bilateral relations often deter states from fully cooperating with universal jurisdiction cases. This unspoken pressure can manifest in subtle yet powerful ways, subtly discouraging the sharing of evidence or the extradition of suspects, effectively rendering international legal instruments ineffective. States may also prioritize their economic or political interests, choosing to protect their relations with suspected states over the pursuit of international justice.

The consequences of this lack of cooperation are far-reaching. It perpetuates a culture of impunity, signaling to potential perpetrators that they can commit heinous crimes with a reasonable expectation of escaping punishment. This not only undermines the rule of law on a global scale but also directly impacts the victims of these crimes, who are denied the opportunity for redress and justice. Such a system ultimately fails to meet the fundamental principles of accountability and justice that underpins the very concept of universal jurisdiction.

Remedying this deficit requires a multi-pronged approach. Strengthening existing international legal frameworks and mechanisms for cooperation is crucial. This includes streamlining extradition processes, developing clear protocols for information sharing, and establishing more effective dispute resolution mechanisms. Furthermore, fostering a culture of international cooperation and mutual respect is essential. States must prioritize the global pursuit of justice over immediate national interests, acknowledging the shared responsibility in combating international crimes. This will require open dialogues, capacity building initiatives, and a sustained commitment to uphold international legal norms. Ultimately, the effectiveness of universal jurisdiction hinges not just on its legal foundation but also on the genuine cooperation among states in applying it. Without a concerted effort towards greater collaboration, the promise of universal jurisdiction will remain unfulfilled, leaving victims without justice and perpetrators without accountability.

4.5 Judicial Capacity

Judicial capacity presents a significant hurdle to the effective implementation of universal jurisdiction. Without robust judicial systems capable of handling complex international criminal cases, the principle remains largely theoretical. This deficiency is not simply a matter of insufficient numbers of judges; it encompasses a broader range of issues including specialized training, adequate resources, and the presence of a legal infrastructure that supports such complex proceedings. This lack of capacity can manifest itself in various ways, from lengthy delays in processing cases to outright dismissals due to procedural inadequacies.

The problem extends beyond simply having enough judges. These cases often require expertise in international law, human rights law, and evidence gathering techniques specific to transnational crimes. Judges need extensive training in these areas to adequately assess evidence, understand the intricacies of international legal instruments, and apply the appropriate legal standards. Further, the investigation and prosecution of these crimes require significant financial resources to support investigative teams, expert witnesses, translation services, and the overall logistical demands of international trials. Many states, particularly developing nations, lack the financial capacity to invest in this area. This financial burden often falls disproportionately on the states that are most willing to uphold the principle of universal jurisdiction, creating an imbalance that impacts the system's efficacy.

Investigative capacity is equally crucial. Effective prosecution depends heavily on robust investigations that can gather sufficient, credible evidence to support a conviction. This involves significant logistical challenges, often spanning multiple countries and requiring coordination with foreign authorities. The successful prosecution of these cases often necessitates collaboration between various states, including the sharing of evidence, witness protection programs, and mutual legal assistance. However, many states lack the internal mechanisms or the political will to support such international cooperation. A lack of coordination can lead to fragmented investigations, weakened prosecutions, and ultimately, the failure to hold perpetrators accountable. The complexity of the investigative process itself, often involving intricate financial transactions, sophisticated technologies, or cross-border criminal networks, adds to the challenge.

Beyond the need for adequate funding and training, judicial capacity also necessitates procedural fairness and adherence to international human rights standards. The accused must be afforded all the protections guaranteed under international law, including the right to a fair trial, legal representation, and due process. This requires judges and court systems to be capable of navigating the intricacies of these rights while maintaining the integrity of the proceedings. Failures in this area can undermine the legitimacy of universal jurisdiction and erode confidence in the international judicial system. A commitment to transparency, efficiency, and fairness, is crucial.

The scarcity of specialized expertise within judicial systems acts as a crucial constraint. The nature of universal jurisdiction cases demands a high level of specialization, encompassing knowledge of international criminal law, human rights law, and various aspects of evidence gathering and presentation in international forums. This creates a need for highly trained legal professionals and expert witnesses, a demand often outstripped by the available capacity within many states. It creates a bottleneck for the entire judicial process. The dearth of qualified professionals capable of handling these complex cases frequently results in significant delays and potentially flawed judgments. The resulting backlog of cases further contributes to the overall problem of weak judicial capacity.

Moreover, the lack of judicial infrastructure itself often hinders the effective implementation of universal jurisdiction. This encompasses the availability of appropriate court facilities, translation services, and the necessary technological support for managing evidence and conducting cross-border legal proceedings. Many states lack the necessary infrastructure to accommodate such complex and resource-intensive cases. The absence of these crucial support systems can dramatically impede the efficient and effective administration of justice, creating further complications. The resulting delays and challenges often negatively impact the outcome of the trials themselves.

In conclusion, strengthening judicial capacity is not merely a matter of increasing the number of judges; it requires a comprehensive and multi-faceted approach. Significant investments in training, resources, infrastructure, and international cooperation are needed to create truly effective judicial systems capable of handling the complexities of universal jurisdiction cases. Without such a commitment, the principle will continue to face significant challenges in its implementation, undermining its potential to promote global criminal accountability.

5 Contemporary Cases & Impacts

The Pinochet case, arguably the most influential application of universal jurisdiction, dramatically shifted the landscape of international criminal law. His arrest in London in 1998, based on a Spanish arrest warrant for crimes against humanity committed in Chile, sparked intense debate and legal maneuvering. While ultimately unsuccessful in securing his conviction in the UK, the case demonstrated the potential for domestic courts to assert jurisdiction over heinous crimes committed abroad, regardless of the perpetrator's nationality or the location of the offense. This bold assertion challenged traditional notions of state sovereignty and spurred further exploration of the principle's viability. The subsequent legal battles, appeals, and international discussions surrounding the Pinochet case helped to refine the legal framework governing universal jurisdiction, clarifying its scope and limitations in practice. This case firmly established the possibility that even heads of state are not immune from prosecution for international crimes.

The prosecution of Rwandan officials in Belgium for the 1994 genocide, while raising important jurisdictional issues and facing difficulties related to evidence gathering and witness protection, underscored the potential, albeit limited, of universal jurisdiction to achieve a modicum of justice. Cases like these, though fraught with logistical hurdles and political sensitivities, paved the way for the International Criminal Tribunal for Rwanda (ICTR), and importantly, demonstrated the capacity of states to address atrocities through domestic channels even where international cooperation is lacking or unreliable. The challenges faced in these cases, such as obtaining sufficient evidence from unstable or uncooperative countries, continue to underline the need for enhanced international cooperation mechanisms. These early efforts, whilst imperfect, helped shape the evolving jurisprudence around universal jurisdiction.

However, the application of universal jurisdiction hasn't been without setbacks. Several attempts to prosecute individuals for war crimes or crimes against humanity have been unsuccessful. This isn't solely due to lack of evidence. Often, political pressures and jurisdictional disputes have thwarted prosecutions. The legal battles surrounding such cases frequently highlight the conflict between the desire for global accountability and the practical realities of international cooperation. The reluctance of some states to cooperate in investigations or extradition proceedings, along with concerns about the potential for politically motivated prosecutions, poses significant challenges to the effective implementation of universal jurisdiction. Furthermore, capacity building in participating states remains critical for effective implementation.

The impact of universal jurisdiction extends beyond individual prosecutions. It has arguably played a significant role in shaping customary international law, by reinforcing the principle that certain crimes are so egregious that they transcend national boundaries and demand universal accountability. Its influence on the development of international criminal law is undeniable. The very existence of universal jurisdiction, even with its limitations, has heightened awareness of the responsibility of states to address atrocities, thereby contributing to the creation of a norm of accountability. Furthermore, the principle fosters a culture of vigilance against international crimes and encourages a more proactive approach to justice.

The growing body of jurisprudence surrounding universal jurisdiction shows its evolution. While the initial applications focused largely on genocide and crimes against humanity, we're now seeing expansion to cover other international crimes such as war crimes, torture, and terrorism. The evolving nature of international threats and the increasing awareness of transboundary crimes necessitates a broader scope of universal jurisdiction. Yet, this requires careful consideration of the balance between universality and specificity to maintain its legitimacy and effectiveness, as inappropriate extensions might jeopardize its standing.

Nonetheless, the practical challenges are considerable. The absence of a universal criminal court, capable of consistently prosecuting international crimes, means the reliance on individual states can prove inconsistent. This inconsistent application, largely based on domestic legal frameworks and political will, creates unevenness, and hence, injustice. This underscores the need for stronger international cooperation to ensure a more comprehensive and coherent approach to the prosecution of perpetrators of international crimes. Furthermore, the resources needed for investigations, prosecutions, and ensuring due process, are often lacking, particularly in states with limited capacity. This disparity underlines the fundamental issue of uneven playing fields and further emphasizes the need for capacity building and the allocation of international funding to support states actively pursuing universal jurisdiction cases.

The future of universal jurisdiction hinges on addressing these challenges. Greater international cooperation is paramount, including the sharing of information and resources, harmonization of legal frameworks, and enhanced coordination among national judiciaries and international bodies. Strengthening international mechanisms for witness protection and evidence gathering is equally critical, to ensure that prosecutions are both credible and effective. Increased efforts toward capacity building in states with limited resources are essential for enhancing their capability in handling these complex and demanding cases. A collaborative, comprehensive approach is necessary to ensure that universal jurisdiction becomes a truly effective tool for achieving global criminal accountability. Only through dedicated international cooperation and resource allocation can the promise of universal jurisdiction be fully realized.

5.1 Notable Prosecutions

The Pinochet case, arguably the most impactful application of universal jurisdiction, dramatically shifted the landscape of international criminal law. His arrest in London in 1998, based on a Spanish warrant for crimes against humanity committed in Chile, sent shockwaves through the international community. The ensuing legal battles, which spanned years and involved multiple jurisdictions, highlighted both the potential and the complexities inherent in this principle. The ultimate outcome, while not resulting in his conviction in Spain due to his deteriorating health, established a significant precedent: even former heads of state are not immune from prosecution for grave international crimes. This case served as a powerful symbol, underscoring that impunity for such atrocities is unacceptable and that universal jurisdiction offers a crucial avenue for accountability. The global reverberations were undeniable, inspiring other nations to consider pursuing similar actions against perpetrators of international crimes, significantly shaping future jurisprudence.

The prosecution of Charles Taylor, former President of Liberia, before the Special Court for Sierra Leone, represented a groundbreaking achievement in international criminal justice. While not strictly a case of universal jurisdiction, as the court was established by a UN Security Council resolution, it nevertheless demonstrated the growing international commitment to holding individuals accountable for war crimes, crimes against humanity, and other atrocities. The trial itself was lengthy and complex, involving numerous witnesses and extensive evidence. Taylor's conviction, though ultimately appealed, represented a monumental step towards dismantling the pervasive culture of impunity surrounding armed conflicts. His actions—supporting rebel groups and using brutal tactics to maintain power—were meticulously examined, resulting in a landmark judgment reinforcing the importance of individual criminal responsibility for even the highest-ranking officials. This marked a significant triumph for international justice, signaling a growing determination to prosecute those responsible for atrocities even amidst chaotic conflict.

Examining the case of Agathe Uwilingiyimana, the Rwandan Prime Minister who was brutally murdered during the 1994 genocide, provides a stark contrast. Despite compelling evidence of her assassination and the broader context of the genocide, bringing those responsible to justice through universal jurisdiction proved challenging. While various countries explored the possibility of prosecution, logistical and jurisdictional hurdles, including securing sufficient evidence and cooperation from involved states, significantly hindered progress. This illustrates the practical limitations that frequently hamper the effective application of universal jurisdiction. The inability to prosecute, despite a clear moral imperative, exposed the difficulties of applying this principle in complex geopolitical scenarios, where domestic considerations often outweigh the desire for international justice. The case serves as a cautionary tale, highlighting the need for improved international cooperation and stronger mechanisms for evidence gathering and witness protection.

Several other notable prosecutions, while perhaps less publicized than those mentioned, have quietly yet significantly contributed to the evolving jurisprudence of universal jurisdiction. Consider the various cases prosecuted in Belgium, Argentina, Spain, and Germany, involving individuals accused of crimes against humanity and war crimes committed in different regions of the world. These prosecutions, although often met with political resistance and facing intricate legal challenges, gradually established important legal precedents and broadened the understanding of this principle's scope. The cumulative effect of these cases underscores the growing acceptance of universal jurisdiction as a legitimate tool for combating impunity and advancing global criminal accountability, even if the practical difficulties remain substantial. These less widely known prosecutions collectively represent a crucial pillar in the development of the complex legal framework surrounding universal jurisdiction.

Beyond the specific cases, it's crucial to acknowledge the broader impact of these prosecutions. They collectively demonstrate the ongoing evolution of international criminal law, the increasing willingness of certain states to assert universal jurisdiction, and the growing recognition of the fundamental importance of accountability for the most serious international crimes. These legal battles—fought often with perseverance and ingenuity against obstacles of political expediency, jurisdictional constraints, and resource scarcity—have, cumulatively, helped to strengthen international norms against impunity. While challenges remain, these notable prosecutions contribute to a steadily growing body of case law, providing valuable guidance for future efforts to hold perpetrators of grave international crimes accountable. The ongoing pursuit of justice for victims of atrocities relies significantly on the precedents set by these cases, furthering the development of robust international mechanisms for enforcing accountability.

5.2 Impact on International Law

Universal jurisdiction, while conceptually powerful, profoundly impacts international law in several significant ways. Its very existence challenges the traditional notions of state sovereignty, suggesting that certain crimes transcend national boundaries and demand accountability irrespective of where they occurred or the nationality of the perpetrator. This inherent challenge has fueled ongoing debates and legal interpretations, constantly reshaping the landscape of international legal norms.

The exercise of universal jurisdiction necessitates a re-evaluation of jurisdictional principles. Traditional notions of territoriality and nationality are stretched, even superseded, when a state asserts jurisdiction over crimes committed elsewhere by individuals not subject to its national laws. This necessitates a careful balancing act, ensuring that the assertion of universal jurisdiction aligns with established principles of international law, such as the prohibition of arbitrary arrests and detentions, and the right to a fair trial. The development of international legal frameworks capable of mediating such complex jurisdictional disputes is crucial and ongoing.

Furthermore, the application of universal jurisdiction has driven the development of international criminal law itself. The very act of prosecuting individuals for crimes against humanity, genocide, or war crimes under this principle has strengthened the international legal norms that define and prohibit these acts. Cases utilizing universal jurisdiction help establish precedents, clarifying the elements of these crimes and offering valuable jurisprudence that informs future prosecutions, both within the framework of universal jurisdiction and through other international criminal mechanisms. This iterative process leads to a gradual yet substantial refinement of international law in crucial areas.

However, the impact extends beyond the direct application of the law. The mere possibility of prosecution under universal jurisdiction acts as a powerful deterrent, potentially influencing the behavior of states and individuals alike. The knowledge that actions deemed egregious under international law could result in prosecution regardless of geographical location or national refuge creates a layer of accountability that surpasses traditional constraints. This implicit influence on state behavior is a subtle but equally significant consequence of the principle's existence, pushing for greater compliance with international norms. The extent to which this deterrent effect is effective remains a subject of scholarly debate, but its potential impact is undeniable.

The principle also fosters greater cooperation among states, albeit unevenly. Successful prosecutions frequently necessitate international collaboration, requiring states to share information, provide evidence, and potentially even extradite suspects. While challenges to cooperation remain, particularly with states reluctant to relinquish sovereignty, the very process of engaging in these forms of international cooperation for the pursuit of justice helps to build relationships and mechanisms that could prove useful in addressing other international legal issues. This strengthens the multilateral system of international law and fosters a sense of shared responsibility in upholding global justice.

Yet, the impact of universal jurisdiction isn't uniformly positive. Critics raise concerns about potential abuse, the potential for politicization of prosecutions, and the risk of undermining state sovereignty excessively. The uneven application of universal jurisdiction across different states and the varying capacity of judicial systems to handle complex international criminal cases further complicates the picture. These inherent tensions highlight the ongoing need for careful consideration, robust legal frameworks, and improved cooperation amongst states to prevent any misuse or negative consequences. The ongoing discussion and evolution surrounding universal jurisdiction showcases its continuous and multifaceted effect on international law, requiring constant refinement and vigilance to balance its positive potential with the challenges it presents. Addressing these concerns is essential for maximizing the benefits of universal jurisdiction while mitigating potential risks. Careful consideration of these concerns will be crucial for ensuring the long-term viability and effectiveness of universal jurisdiction as a tool for advancing global criminal accountability. The continuous dialogue and refinement of this principle, as well as the collaborative efforts to address its challenges, are paramount to its sustained contribution to the evolution of international law. The principle remains a dynamic and evolving component of the international legal landscape, its impacts continuously shaping the global pursuit of justice. Navigating these complexities requires a nuanced understanding of its potential benefits and challenges, fostering informed discussions and collaboration among states. Only through this ongoing process can the promise of universal jurisdiction be fully realized while safeguarding fundamental principles of international law.

6 Future Directions

The effective application of universal jurisdiction hinges on robust international cooperation. Strengthening this cooperation requires a multi-pronged approach. Firstly, we need formalized agreements between states, clearly outlining procedures for information sharing, evidence gathering, and witness protection. Secondly, the creation of a dedicated international body, perhaps under the auspices of the UN, to facilitate these collaborations is crucial. This body could provide technical assistance, coordinate investigations, and ensure consistent application of legal standards across different jurisdictions. Finally, fostering trust and mutual respect among nations is paramount. This involves diplomatic efforts, capacity-building initiatives, and regular dialogue to address concerns and build consensus around the principles of universal jurisdiction.

A significant obstacle to universal jurisdiction's effectiveness is the persistent problem of impunity. Many perpetrators of grave international crimes operate with a sense of security, knowing prosecution is unlikely. To combat this, targeted sanctions against individuals and entities implicated in such crimes are necessary. These sanctions, which could include asset freezes, travel bans, and arms embargoes, must be effectively enforced by member states, ideally with a UN Security Council resolution to provide broader legitimacy and encourage cooperation. Furthermore, the establishment of international mechanisms for asset recovery – to compensate victims and fund future investigations – can enhance the deterrent effect of these legal mechanisms. We must make it clear that there are severe consequences for the commission of these heinous acts.

The legal framework underpinning universal jurisdiction needs further refinement. The current ambiguity surrounding issues like the definition of 'universal jurisdiction', the specific crimes covered, and the burden of proof create challenges for its effective application. This requires a concerted effort by international legal scholars and practitioners to develop clearer guidelines and standards. International courts and tribunals should play a crucial role in this process, issuing authoritative rulings that clarify ambiguities and establish precedents. Furthermore, greater clarity on the principles of complementarity, that is, the relationship between national and international courts in exercising universal jurisdiction, is needed. Clear lines of authority can prevent conflicts and ensure efficient and effective prosecution.

While considerable progress has been made, significant resource constraints continue to hinder the implementation of universal jurisdiction. Many states, particularly developing nations, lack the financial and human resources necessary to investigate and prosecute complex international crimes. Addressing this disparity requires increased funding from developed countries and international organizations. This funding should support capacity-building programs for judicial and law enforcement agencies in developing states. Such initiatives can encompass training on investigative techniques, evidence gathering, international law, and the specifics of universal jurisdiction. Further, technical assistance in the areas of forensic science and cybercrime investigations could be instrumental in prosecuting offenders effectively.

Ultimately, the future of universal jurisdiction relies on a multifaceted strategy. Strengthening international cooperation, addressing impunity, refining the legal framework, and tackling resource constraints are all essential components of this strategy. However, it also necessitates a change in mind-set. We must move beyond mere rhetorical support for universal jurisdiction and translate commitments into concrete actions, fostering a global culture of accountability and ensuring that those who perpetrate grave international crimes are brought to justice, irrespective of their location or power. This collective effort demands a long-term commitment from states, international organizations, and civil society organizations. Only through sustained engagement and a shared dedication to justice can we hope to fully realize the potential of universal jurisdiction in achieving global criminal accountability.

6.1 Strengthening Mechanisms

Effective implementation of universal jurisdiction hinges on robust mechanisms that overcome inherent challenges. Strengthening these mechanisms requires a multi-faceted approach, focusing on bolstering international cooperation, enhancing judicial capacity, and addressing resource constraints. Without concerted effort in these areas, the potential of universal jurisdiction to hold perpetrators of egregious crimes accountable will remain unrealized.

International cooperation is paramount. States must commit to actively sharing information, providing mutual legal assistance, and coordinating investigations and prosecutions. Agreements facilitating extradition and witness protection programs are crucial. Furthermore, the establishment of a dedicated international body to coordinate investigations and assist national judiciaries would dramatically improve the effectiveness of universal jurisdiction. Such an organization could pool resources, provide technical assistance, and share best practices, overcoming many of the practical limitations currently hindering progress.

Judicial capacity requires significant investment. Training programs for judges and prosecutors specializing in international criminal law are essential. This training must encompass both substantive law and procedural aspects, including evidence gathering, witness examination, and cross-border legal processes. Furthermore, the development of standardized evidentiary rules and procedures is vital to ensure consistency and fairness across jurisdictions. These initiatives will equip national courts with the expertise and tools needed to handle complex international criminal cases effectively.

Resource limitations pose a significant obstacle. Many states lack the financial and human resources necessary to effectively investigate and prosecute international crimes. International financial assistance, targeted at strengthening national judicial systems and providing investigative support, is therefore crucial. This support could include funding for specialized training, equipment procurement, and expert witness testimony. Furthermore, donor states should prioritize funding initiatives aimed at bolstering the capacity of national institutions to investigate and prosecute cases effectively, while respecting national sovereignty and judicial independence.

Addressing impunity necessitates a sustained commitment to tackling the root causes of international crimes. This requires comprehensive strategies involving not only the prosecution of individuals but also tackling systemic issues, such as corruption, human rights abuses, and armed conflict. Moreover, initiatives focused on transitional justice, such as truth commissions and reparations programs, can play a vital role in restoring victims' rights and addressing broader societal harms caused by these crimes.

Strengthening mechanisms also requires addressing political obstacles, which often hinder cooperation and hamper effective prosecutions. Diplomatic initiatives fostering dialogue and building consensus amongst states are essential. Increased transparency and accountability in the handling of international crime cases could encourage greater international cooperation. Regular reporting mechanisms, overseen by an international body, could help to monitor progress and identify areas needing further attention. Creating an international body to actively encourage cooperation could also help break down some of these political barriers.

The development and implementation of a comprehensive strategy involving these interwoven mechanisms is essential for enhancing universal jurisdiction. This multifaceted approach requires a commitment from states, international organizations, and civil society. Only through such concerted effort can we effectively hold perpetrators of international crimes accountable and advance the pursuit of global criminal accountability. Without this coordinated, comprehensive effort, universal jurisdiction will remain a potent ideal but a weak instrument in the fight against impunity. The consequences of inaction are significant and far-reaching; a world where serious international crimes go unpunished risks undermining the rule of law and international peace and security. Therefore, strengthening these mechanisms is not merely a matter of legal refinement but a vital step in establishing a more just and equitable global order.

6.2 Expanding Cooperation

Effective international cooperation is paramount for the successful application of universal jurisdiction. Without robust collaboration between states, the pursuit of justice for egregious international crimes remains severely hampered. This necessitates a multi-pronged approach, focusing on fostering trust, streamlining information sharing, and strengthening mutual legal assistance mechanisms. Judicial training programs, specifically tailored to the complexities of universal jurisdiction, can help standardize procedures and ensure a consistent interpretation of international law across jurisdictions. These initiatives are not merely beneficial, but vital to the overall success of the system.

The exchange of evidence and witness testimony often presents a significant hurdle. Discrepancies in legal systems and evidentiary standards frequently complicate cross-border investigations. Harmonizing these differences, through bilateral agreements and multilateral treaties, can significantly reduce these obstacles. Moreover, the establishment of specialized international units dedicated to facilitating evidence transfer can expedite investigations and prosecutions. Such cooperation is not merely desirable; it's an essential component in bringing perpetrators to justice. A coordinated and efficient system is absolutely crucial for effectively pursuing global criminal accountability.

Political will is often the most critical yet elusive element in achieving international cooperation. States must prioritize the interests of justice over nationalistic agendas or political expediency. This requires a fundamental shift in perspective – a recognition that accountability for international crimes is not merely a matter of national jurisdiction but a collective responsibility of the international community. This is more than just a legal issue; it is a crucial step in establishing a world where serious crimes are not shielded by national boundaries. Only through concerted efforts and a shared commitment to justice can we hope to effectively deter these atrocities.

Financial constraints frequently impede the ability of states to participate fully in universal jurisdiction proceedings. Many nations, particularly those with limited resources, struggle to fund investigations, extraditions, and participation in international trials. The international community should actively support these states through targeted funding, capacity-building programs, and technical assistance. This assistance must be structured strategically, ensuring that it addresses specific needs and enhances the investigative and judicial capabilities of participating nations. Focusing on resource allocation and equitable distribution is vital to ensuring effective implementation of universal jurisdiction's principles.

Beyond financial support, technology plays an increasingly significant role in facilitating international cooperation. Secure communication platforms and digital evidence sharing systems are crucial for efficient investigation and prosecution. Investment in these technologies is critical, not just for enhancing communication but also for ensuring the integrity and security of the evidence involved in these complex cases. The right resources, coupled with streamlined processes, are fundamental in ensuring universal jurisdiction delivers on its promise.

The development of robust mechanisms for monitoring and evaluating cooperation is necessary. Regular assessments of inter-state collaboration efforts can identify areas of success and those needing improvement. Such evaluations should be transparent and inclusive, engaging stakeholders at all levels of the judicial process. This monitoring is essential not only to track progress but to provide valuable feedback for adjusting strategies and resource allocation. Continuous improvement is vital for the evolving nature of international crime and the complex legal landscape.

Finally, fostering a culture of accountability extends beyond formal legal mechanisms. This requires a commitment to educating the public and raising awareness about international crimes and the importance of universal jurisdiction. Promoting a culture of collaboration and shared responsibility within the international community is crucial for long-term success. These efforts, encompassing education, awareness-building, and collaborative initiatives, are integral to creating a world where impunity for international crimes is ultimately eradicated. The future of international justice depends on this collective commitment.

6.3 Addressing Impunity

Impunity, the escape from justice, remains a persistent obstacle to achieving global criminal accountability. It fuels cycles of violence, undermining the rule of law and fostering a climate of fear where perpetrators of atrocities believe they can act with impunity. This pervasive problem necessitates a multifaceted approach that transcends the limitations of individual states and embraces the collaborative potential of the international community. Addressing impunity requires a fundamental shift in mindset, moving beyond reactive measures to proactively prevent the commission of crimes and ensure that those who do perpetrate them are held accountable, regardless of their position or power. Effective strategies must incorporate robust investigative capacities, strengthened judicial institutions, and unwavering political will.

The successful prosecution of individuals under universal jurisdiction often hinges on the availability of robust evidence. Gathering and preserving evidence from conflict zones or areas lacking stability presents significant challenges. International cooperation is crucial here, requiring a network of trained investigators, secure evidence storage facilities, and collaborative information-sharing mechanisms. However, this network must be built upon mutual trust and respect between states, overcoming political obstacles and geopolitical considerations that can hinder evidence-gathering efforts. Additionally, protecting witnesses and ensuring their safety is equally paramount, requiring comprehensive witness protection programs and secure communication channels.

Judicial capacity, particularly within states willing to exercise universal jurisdiction, is another critical factor. Courts require specialized training and resources to effectively handle complex international crimes cases. This includes expertise in international law, evidence gathering techniques specific to international crimes, and the ability to deal with sensitive information that might affect international relations and national security. Funding is often insufficient, leaving courts understaffed and ill-equipped to handle the complex demands of these cases. Investing in judicial training, infrastructure, and technological resources is therefore a vital step towards ensuring effective prosecution.

Political will, unfortunately, often proves to be the most significant hurdle. Universal jurisdiction can be a politically sensitive topic, particularly for states concerned about potential repercussions on their own national security or foreign relations. This often involves navigating complex geopolitical tensions and prioritizing national interests over international justice. Encouraging states to uphold their commitments under international law requires diplomatic pressure, public awareness campaigns, and robust mechanisms for accountability. International organizations and civil society groups can play an instrumental role in advocating for the implementation of universal jurisdiction and holding states accountable for their failures to do so.

Beyond prosecution, addressing impunity requires a comprehensive approach to prevention. This means promoting the rule of law at the national level, strengthening international norms against impunity, and supporting transitional justice initiatives in post-conflict settings. Transitional justice mechanisms, such as truth commissions and reparations programs, are vital to addressing past atrocities and fostering reconciliation. Strengthening international cooperation in these areas, including technical assistance and financial support to states working towards transitional justice, is a key component of this preventative approach. The emphasis should shift from simply prosecuting perpetrators to creating societies where the commission of such crimes is actively discouraged and prevented through robust legal frameworks and supportive institutions. Only through such a comprehensive, multi-faceted, and collaborative approach can we hope to significantly reduce impunity and advance the cause of global criminal accountability.

7 Conclusion: The Path Forward

The journey towards universal jurisdiction's full realization has been, and continues to be, a complex and often arduous one. Progress has been made, undeniably, marked by landmark prosecutions and evolving legal frameworks. However, significant hurdles remain, demanding sustained effort and innovative solutions from the international community. The uneven application of universal jurisdiction highlights the persistent influence of political considerations and the stark reality of unequal resource distribution among nations.

Addressing impunity for heinous international crimes requires a multi-faceted approach. Simply increasing the number of prosecutions, while crucial, is insufficient without addressing systemic issues like the lack of robust international cooperation mechanisms. States must actively commit to sharing information, providing evidence, and ensuring the smooth extradition of suspects, irrespective of political sensitivities. Furthermore, the development of standardized legal procedures and training programs for judicial officials across various jurisdictions is paramount to ensure consistency and fairness in the application of universal jurisdiction.

Judicial capacity building within states, particularly in developing nations, is another critical area requiring attention. Investing in training programs for judges, prosecutors, and investigators will improve the quality of investigations and prosecutions, ultimately leading to more successful outcomes.

This involves not just technical legal training, but also the cultivation of ethical considerations and an understanding of the cultural nuances surrounding crimes that often cross borders. Financial and technical assistance from wealthier nations will be crucial to support these initiatives. Without addressing this gap in resources, the goal of truly universal jurisdiction remains an unattainable ideal.

The ongoing debate surrounding the limits of universal jurisdiction, particularly concerning state sovereignty, necessitates careful navigation. Striking a balance between the need for global accountability and the legitimate concerns of individual states is a delicate act. The principle of complementarity, where international courts only intervene when domestic systems fail to pursue justice, remains a vital safeguard against unilateral action. Nonetheless, efforts to codify and clarify the parameters of universal jurisdiction will further mitigate potential conflicts and improve its predictability.

International collaboration remains the cornerstone of effective universal jurisdiction. Strengthening existing partnerships and forging new alliances between nations, international organizations, and NGOs is essential. Joint investigation teams, collaborative prosecution strategies, and shared databases of evidence can greatly enhance the effectiveness of universal jurisdiction and deter future atrocities. The establishment of a dedicated international body to coordinate efforts and facilitate information exchange could prove particularly valuable in this endeavor. Such a body would act as a central hub, promoting best practices and ensuring the coordinated application of universal jurisdiction globally.

Looking ahead, several key questions warrant further consideration. How can the international community more effectively address the political obstacles hindering the implementation of universal jurisdiction? What innovative strategies can be employed to overcome resource constraints and ensure equitable access to justice? Furthermore, how can the principle of universal jurisdiction be effectively integrated into existing international legal frameworks, such as the Rome Statute of the International Criminal

Court, to create a more cohesive and efficient system of global criminal accountability? These questions, and many others, require ongoing investigation and vigorous debate among legal scholars, policymakers, and practitioners. The path toward global criminal accountability, guided by the principle of universal jurisdiction, is a long and winding one, but with persistent dedication and strategic cooperation, it is a path that we must continue to tread. The pursuit of justice demands nothing less.

7.1 Assessing Progress

Measuring the effectiveness of universal jurisdiction is a complex undertaking. Success isn't simply a matter of counting prosecutions; it's about understanding the broader impact on international criminal law, the deterrent effect, and the evolving understanding of state sovereignty. A purely quantitative approach would be misleading, potentially ignoring the subtle, yet significant, shifts in international norms and legal interpretations fostered by even unsuccessful attempts to prosecute. We must consider the ripple effects.

Focusing solely on convictions ignores the strategic value of initiating proceedings. The very act of bringing a case, even if ultimately unsuccessful due to jurisdictional challenges or lack of evidence, can send a powerful message, potentially impacting the behaviour of future perpetrators. Such a case also contributes to the body of legal precedent, shaping future jurisprudence. Moreover, the process itself, including investigative efforts and international cooperation, can unearth valuable information, which helps inform subsequent investigations and prosecutions by other entities. The symbolic weight of a case is a substantial factor.

Consider the political context. Successful prosecutions often require a delicate balancing act, navigating complex relationships between states. A prosecution that appears politically motivated, or that disregards concerns about state sovereignty, might achieve a short-term victory but damage long-term efforts to build international cooperation – a crucial ingredient for the successful application of universal jurisdiction. The long-term goal is to establish a system of accountability that is both effective and legitimate, not simply to secure a series of convictions. International support is paramount.

Furthermore, the resources dedicated to universal jurisdiction cases are often limited. This scarcity forces a prioritization process, naturally leading to a selection bias. Cases that are well-resourced and politically feasible receive more attention, perhaps overlooking cases of equal or even greater gravity due to lack of capacity. This naturally creates disparities in the types of cases prosecuted, a problem which necessitates a deeper analysis beyond simple case counts. This requires a more nuanced interpretation of available data.

The impact of universal jurisdiction extends beyond individual prosecutions. Its development and use are influencing international law, shaping international legal discourse, and fostering a growing awareness of the need for accountability for egregious human rights violations. This evolution of norms and expectations is a significant, though difficult to quantify, success. Moreover, this evolution can act as a catalyst for domestic legal reforms within nations, pushing them to confront their own roles in perpetuating impunity. This is a crucial aspect of the overall impact.

Ultimately, assessing progress requires a multi-faceted approach. We must move beyond simple metrics like conviction rates and consider the broader consequences, including the development of international legal norms, the deterrent effects, the promotion of international cooperation, and the creation of a more just and equitable global order. Future research should focus on developing more sophisticated methods for measuring these indirect, yet profoundly important, consequences, drawing on diverse data sources and analytical techniques. A comprehensive evaluation demands a systematic approach.

A robust assessment necessitates a comparative analysis across different jurisdictions and legal systems. The effectiveness of universal jurisdiction can vary greatly depending on factors such as the legal framework, judicial independence, and the level of political will. By comparing successes and failures across different contexts, we can gain valuable insights into what factors contribute to successful implementation and how potential shortcomings might be addressed. Comparative studies are essential.

The challenge lies in developing reliable and consistent methods for measuring the impact of universal jurisdiction, accounting for the complexities of international law and the interplay of political, legal, and social factors. This will inevitably require interdisciplinary collaboration between legal scholars, political scientists, and social scientists, combining quantitative and qualitative research methods. Collaboration is key. The pursuit of global criminal accountability is a continuous process, not a destination. We must acknowledge the ongoing evolution.

Looking forward, we need to refine our understanding of how universal jurisdiction interacts with other mechanisms for international justice, such as international criminal tribunals and hybrid courts. Understanding their complementarity and potential conflicts is crucial for maximizing their effectiveness. This holistic view is critical for optimizing the pursuit of justice. A more efficient coordination, a collaborative strategy, are essential for global accountability. This requires more detailed research and analyses.

Moreover, ongoing challenges, such as resource constraints and the need for stronger international cooperation, necessitate innovative solutions and a commitment from the international community. Strengthening judicial capacity in states willing to prosecute these crimes is essential, in addition to building a more robust system for evidence gathering and sharing across borders. A well-structured framework, providing support and funding, is vital for global criminal accountability. The path ahead requires a collaborative and resolute approach.

7.2 Looking Ahead

The pursuit of global criminal accountability through universal jurisdiction remains a complex and evolving undertaking. While significant strides have been made, considerable hurdles persist. Success hinges not merely on legal frameworks but also on robust political will and sustained international collaboration. Without a concerted effort to overcome these challenges, the promise of universal jurisdiction will remain largely unfulfilled, leaving countless victims of heinous crimes without recourse to justice. We must, therefore, look towards strengthening existing mechanisms and fostering a more cooperative international environment.

Effective implementation demands more than just legal pronouncements; it necessitates practical strategies for investigation, prosecution, and witness protection. Consider the resource disparities between states: some possess well-equipped investigative agencies and robust judicial systems, while others lack the fundamental infrastructure to even begin to address these complex cases. Bridging this gap requires meaningful investment in capacity building, training programs, and technology transfer, ensuring that all states, regardless of their resources, are equipped to participate in this global endeavor. A truly universal system cannot be built on uneven foundations.

International cooperation is paramount. The sharing of information, evidence, and expertise across borders is essential for successful prosecutions. However, political obstacles often impede this crucial exchange. States may be reluctant to cooperate with investigations or extraditions, driven by concerns about national sovereignty or political expediency. Overcoming this reticence requires a significant shift in mindset, promoting a shared understanding that accountability for international crimes transcends national borders and serves the interests of the international community as a whole. The establishment of clearer guidelines and mechanisms for facilitating cooperation, perhaps through international legal instruments or dedicated institutions, could be vital.

The issue of impunity, the widespread failure to bring perpetrators to justice, remains a significant obstacle. Many perpetrators of international crimes operate with a sense of immunity, confident that they will escape accountability. This stems from a variety of factors, including weak enforcement mechanisms, lack of political will, and jurisdictional complexities. Addressing impunity demands a multifaceted approach, focusing on strengthening investigative capacities, enhancing the effectiveness of international criminal tribunals, and promoting a culture of accountability where perpetrators understand that their actions will have consequences, irrespective of their location or power. The road ahead is long and requires a global commitment.

Looking ahead, the focus should be on refining existing mechanisms and forging new collaborations. This includes exploring innovative strategies for evidence gathering and preservation in conflict zones or situations where state institutions are weak or collapsed. Likewise, it requires investing in the training of legal professionals, investigators, and judges specialized in international criminal law, equipping them with the skills and knowledge to navigate the complexities of these cases. This involves not just technical expertise, but also a deep understanding of the ethical and political dimensions of pursuing justice in a globalized world.

Furthermore, the future of universal jurisdiction requires a robust and accessible system of victim support and reparations. Victims often suffer not only physical and psychological trauma but also significant financial losses and social disruption. Providing them with adequate support and opportunities for redress is crucial for achieving restorative justice and promoting reconciliation. This means not only ensuring that victims have access to legal representation and psychological services, but also establishing mechanisms for financial compensation and restoring their dignity.

Ultimately, the future of universal jurisdiction depends on a collective commitment to upholding the rule of law and promoting global justice. It is a long-term endeavor requiring sustained effort, international cooperation, and a shared vision of a world where perpetrators of heinous crimes are held accountable for their actions, no matter where they are located. The journey towards global criminal accountability is far from over, yet the unwavering pursuit of justice, guided by a commitment to human rights and the principles of universal jurisdiction, offers hope for a more just and equitable future. Only with persistent dedication and innovative strategies can we effectively address these persistent challenges and realize the full potential of universal jurisdiction. We can pave a path forward toward a future where accountability transcends national borders and individuals are held to account for crimes against humanity, irrespective of their status or location. The challenges are significant, but the pursuit of justice demands nothing less than our collective effort.

7.3 Remaining Questions

The inherent tension between state sovereignty and the imperative for global justice remains a central dilemma. While universal jurisdiction offers a powerful tool to prosecute perpetrators of heinous international crimes, its effectiveness hinges on robust international cooperation, something often elusive in practice. Can we realistically expect states, particularly powerful ones, to consistently prioritize universal jurisdiction over their own national interests? The potential for political manipulation and selective enforcement further complicates the issue. How do we ensure that the application of universal jurisdiction is equitable and doesn't become a tool for targeting political opponents? These are not merely academic questions; they are crucial for the principle's legitimacy and long-term viability.

The practical limitations of universal jurisdiction are substantial. Prosecuting these complex cases often requires extensive resources, specialized expertise, and substantial time commitments. Many states, particularly those with less developed legal systems or limited resources, lack the capacity to effectively investigate and prosecute such crimes. Furthermore, the gathering of evidence across national borders often proves immensely challenging. Witness protection, securing physical evidence, and navigating differing legal systems all present formidable hurdles. How can the international community provide effective support to states seeking to exercise universal jurisdiction, bridging the resource gap and improving investigative capacities? Addressing these practical constraints is vital to the principle's success.

A significant challenge lies in the inconsistent application of universal jurisdiction across different states and jurisdictions. Some states readily embrace the principle while others actively resist it, creating a fragmented and uneven system of accountability. This inconsistency weakens the overall impact of universal jurisdiction and raises questions about its fairness and legitimacy. Furthermore, the lack of a unified international body or mechanism to coordinate the application of universal jurisdiction exacerbates these problems. How can we create a more standardized and predictable approach, fostering greater harmonization in the application of this vital legal principle across all nations?

The issue of complementarity also deserves closer scrutiny. The principle of complementarity, which stipulates that universal jurisdiction should only be exercised when domestic courts are unwilling or unable to prosecute, is essential to avoiding jurisdictional conflicts. However, the interpretation and application of complementarity vary widely, potentially leading to inconsistent outcomes. How can we develop clearer criteria for determining when domestic courts are genuinely unwilling or unable to prosecute, preventing abuses and ensuring effective accountability? This remains a complex legal and practical challenge requiring careful consideration. The definition of "unwilling" or "unable" needs more clarity to improve the efficacy of this safeguard.

Looking forward, the future of universal jurisdiction rests on addressing these remaining questions. Enhanced international cooperation is paramount; establishing robust mechanisms for information sharing, witness protection, and evidence gathering is essential. Strengthening the capacity of national judiciaries, particularly in developing nations, will also be crucial. Furthermore, exploring alternative mechanisms for accountability, such as international criminal tribunals or hybrid courts, may be necessary in situations where national courts are demonstrably unable or unwilling to act. Ultimately, the ongoing evolution of universal jurisdiction requires continuous dialogue, collaboration, and a commitment to ensuring that those responsible for egregious international crimes are held to account, regardless of where they may flee. The pursuit of global criminal accountability, though challenging, is a fundamental pillar of international justice.

www.ingramcontent.com/pod-product-compliance
Lightning Source LLC
LaVergne TN
LVHW022027200926
848481LV00007B/2575